FROM THE SKIES OF PARADISE

HAWAII

Niihau

Kauai

Oahu

Molokai

Lanai

Maui

Hawaii

FROM THE SKIES OF PARADISE

HAWAII

Photography by Douglas Peebles

Written by Chris Cook

Mutual Publishing

PREVIOUS PAGE: *Kauai's Kalalau beach meets the entrance to Honopu valley on the Na Pali coast.*

1   2   3   4   5   6   7   8   9
First Edition October 1990

Printed in Hong Kong
ISBN 0-935180-25-1

Mutual Publishing
2055 North King Street
Honolulu, Hawaii 96819
Telephone (808) 924-7732
Fax (808) 943-1689

C O N T E N T S

From the "deep profound darkness" of the blue Pacific Ocean the Islands of Hawaii emerged eons ago. In time, as poetically recorded in the Hawaiian creation prayer, the *Kumulipo,* volcanic fires thrust mountains of molten lava skyward, one by one, to form a 1,600-mile chain that today stretches from the Big Island's South Point, only 1,100 miles from the Equator, to Kure Atoll facing the North Pacific.

After the fires had cooled, seeds windborne from faraway continents or pushed by ocean currents brought plant life to valleys and beaches rich with fertile, mineral-laden, life-giving volcanic soil.

The first creatures to see the islands' splendor were the sea birds, the tiny bats, the whales, a few delicate forest birds, and the wide-ranging ocean fish. Then, silently, the Islands waited for the next epoch in their history.

Sea-roving Polynesians discovered Hawaii about fifteen centuries ago. They sailed here in amazingly sophisticated double-hull voyaging canoes from "Havaiki," in the leeward islands of Tahiti.

Hawaii was the final stop on an incredible pilgrimage that may have begun thousands of years earlier in Asia. The early arrivals found a new homeland, where they could be at peace.

While civilizations and dynasties rose and fell in Asia and Europe, Hawaii remained unknown, uncharted, isolated. About A.D.1300 , even the voyaging canoes ceased to arrive from Havaiki.

This isolation ended on January 18, 1778 when Captain James Cook, commanding a two-ship exploratory squadron of the Royal Navy, ordered H.M.S. *Resolution* and *Discovery* to drop anchor off Waimea, Kauai. The previous day, while sailing toward Alaska from Tahiti, he and his crew had sighted Oahu's mountains.

Cook's discovery opened western eyes to Hawaii, especially when his journals were published in London. Cook's often acute reports of things seen in the South Pacific were illuminated with pen and ink drawings by the ship's artist, John Webber, representing the first known responsible effort to picture the South Pacific islands.

A century after Cook, photographers were recording Hawaiian scenes on glass negatives. But until J.C. "Bud" Mars in 1910 took his Curtiss-powered P-18 biplane up for a brief flight over Fort Shafter on Oahu, cameras and cameramen were bound to either land or sea and had only a limited perspective.

Today, flying thousands of feet above Hawaii's lush valleys, fiery volcanoes and reef fringed beaches, is an everyday event. The high-tech helicopter has become a costly, but necessary, accessory for late twentieth-century photographers who seek to capture Hawaii on film.

From the Skies of Paradise Hawaii offers the very best of aerial images taken during hundreds of hours of helicopter flight over the islands.

Douglas Peebles' aerial portraits capture the natural spectacle of Hawaii—from isolated Niihau, across Kauai, Oahu, Molokai, Lanai, Maui and, finally to Hawaii, "the Big Island." They wondrously illustrate the never ending interplay of timeless scenic beauty, constant physical change, and Hawaii's "golden people" that only an aerial perspective can provide.

OAHU

Oahu, which includes Honolulu and its outlying communities, is known as "the gathering place."

Formed when massive ancient lava flows joined the two parallel Waianae and Koolau volcanic ranges, 40-mile-long Oahu is third in size among the islands of Hawaii.

Oahu has a resident population in excess of 800,000, which is about three fourths of the State's total of 1,098,000. Some fifteen percent of Oahu's population consists of military personnel and their dependents assigned for two to four year tours. On any given day over 100,000 of Hawaii's annual six million-plus overseas visitors are on Oahu.

Honolulu is a fantastic place in which to live and work. Its matrix of business and pleasure opportunities ranges from the busy financial center anchored on Bishop Street to the two miles of sunny, visitor-oriented Waikiki Beach. For those so inclined, Waikiki can be a round-the-clock playground.

Business visitors, whether in the city for a convention or stopping over on a trans-Pacific flight, know Honolulu to be a clean, prosperous, tropical, and cosmopolitan alternative to the sprawling mega-cities of Asia and America.

Military personnel often think of Oahu first as America's far western fortress, sometimes only as a port or airfield en route to a new duty post and as a place to visit on the next "R & R" leave. For many, Hawaii is somewhere to make a new home.

Sports enthusiasts flock to Oahu to challenge the incomparable winter surf along the famed North Shore, to guide their sailboards in

PREVIOUS PAGES: *The towering pinnacles of the Koolau Range provide a dramatic setting for the Windward Oahu community of Kaneohe. Mokolii island, "Chinaman's Hat," is a tiny dot in the glassy windward channel.*

LEFT: *Oahu's secluded white sand beaches, explored on foot or in a four-wheel-drive vehicle, offer isolated sunbathing, uncrowded surfing, and views of coral reefs teeming with marine life.*

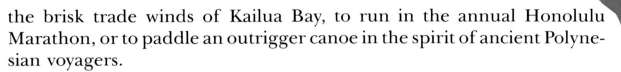

the brisk trade winds of Kailua Bay, to run in the annual Honolulu Marathon, or to paddle an outrigger canoe in the spirit of ancient Polynesian voyagers.

Neighbor Islanders find Honolulu exhilarating—the Big City, a shopping paradise. Students know it as their last glimpse of home as they fly off to a mainland college and as their first contact on return.

"The gathering place" also abounds with history. Beautifully restored Iolani Palace, the only royal palace ever constructed on American soil, recalling the hopeful days of the Hawaiian Kingdom, is the centerpiece of downtown Honolulu.

Next to busy Honolulu International Airport are Hickam Air Force Base and the adjacent Pearl Harbor naval facilities, the targets of the December 1941 Japanese air attack that thrust the United States into World War II.

The relaxed and refurbished Royal Hawaiian and Moana Surfrider Hotels at Waikiki are the ancestors of today's highrise glass and concrete pleasure domes, splendid monuments to glorious days of beach boys, visiting celebrities, luxury steamships and "boat days."

Honolulu has come a long way since 1795 when Kamehameha the Great landed his army from Maui and the Big Island near Waikiki, determined to conquer Oahu. Advancing against desperate resistance, his forces pushed Oahu's warriors back to and off the brink of the Nuuanu Pali. His effective unification of the Hawaiian Kingdom led to the development of today's Hawaii. Appropriately cast in bronze, painted in gold leaf, and often draped in flowers, Kamehameha watches over the city from a pedestal facing Iolani Palace in downtown Honolulu.

Cruise ships still tie up at Aloha Tower. The tallest building in Hawaii when constructed in 1926, the 10-story landmark was the gateway to Hawaii for most pre-jet age visitors . The tower clock still strikes the hours for busy downtown Honolulu.

OPPOSITE: *Popular man-made Magic Island off Ala Moana Beach Park is a favorite retreat of Honolulu beachgoers, fishermen, picnickers, and surfers.*

ABOVE: *The turquoise lagoon and the 30-story-high rainbow mosaic of the Hilton Hawaiian Village are a colorful backdrop to the international fleet berthed at the Ala Wai Boat Harbor.*

15

*Outrigger canoe paddlers
practice on the Ala Wai Canal
as Honolulu golfers swing a
club in the shadow of Waikiki's
high rises at the Ala Wai
course, once rice paddies and
taro patches.*

Gusty trade winds off Diamond Head, Hawaii's most famous landmark, provide optimum conditions for sailboarders. Long a popular surfing spot, Diamond Head Beach is often the site of water sports competitions.

OPPOSITE: *Diamond Head got its name in 1825 when sailors found diamond-like calcite crystals on its slopes. Today, Diamond Head and nearby Kahala are Honolulu's wealthiest neighborhoods. The Kahala Hilton Hotel is on the beach east of Diamond Head.*

ABOVE: *Schools of protected Hawaiian reef fish make the Hanauma Bay Beach Park immensely popular with snorkelers. The waters are a State Marine Preserve. The sheltered, curving bay evokes images of the South Pacific.*

RIGHT: *Makapuu Lighthouse atop a black lava sea cliff at Oahu's most easterly point overlooks Rabbit Island, hang gliders, the bodysurfers at Makapuu Beach Park, Sea Life Park and pastoral Waimanalo.*

OPPOSITE: *The twin Mokulua islands off Lanikai, a charming Windward beachfront community, are a favorite with kayakers. Close-knit Lanikai celebrates its uniqueness at an annual community parade.*

20

ABOVE: *Mount Olomana shadows the banana patches and grazing cattle of verdant Maunawili Valley. The inspiration for Queen Liliuokalani's famous parting song "Aloha 'Oe," the isolated valley and peak are enclaves of old Hawaii in fast-growing Honolulu.*

OPPOSITE: *Downtown Honolulu and Nuuanu Valley peek from behind the Koolau mountains. Thousands of Kailua and Kaneohe commuters daily pass windy Pali Lookout over which Hawaii's King Kamehameha's forces drove Oahu warriors to their deaths 200 years ago.*

Bordered by elegant homes and the Kaneohe Marine Corps Air Station, reef-fringed Kaneohe Bay is alive with sailboats and jet fighters. Tiny Coconut Island has an active laboratory of the Hawaii Institute of Marine Biology. An ancient Hawaiian fishpond is visible at Heeia on the north end of Kaneohe Bay.

Puu Kanehoalani stretches skyward above Kualoa Point Regional Park. Kualoa Ranch, Oahu's largest cattle spread, is a living reminder of Windward Oahu's paniolo *(cowboy) days.*

The quiet Windward community of Kaaawa is known for its Crouching Lion rock formation. Crouching Lion Inn is a far, yet near retreat from the hustle and bustle of Honolulu.

27

ABOVE: *Lovely Kahana Bay is an example of an ancient Hawaiian* ahapuaa *land division which ran from seashore to mountain top and contained everything a village would need. Local families frequently camp along its curving beach.*

OPPOSITE: *With low-rise condominiums next to* taro *fields, Punaluu in rural Windward Oahu clearly reveals the interplay of modern times and the old days.*

OPPOSITE: *Oahu's North Shore is world famed for its miles of perfect surfing amid rural Hawaiian ambience. Professional world surfing championships are decided on the huge waves at Sunset Beach, Banzai Pipeline and Waimea Bay.*

ABOVE: *The Hawaiian Electric Company selected the windy hills above the old sugar mill at Kahuku for a field of experimental windmills. The other-worldly high-tech fans that produce power for energy-hungry Honolulu out-perform most wind energy sites in the United States.*

ABOVE: *In summer the Waimea Bay beach is wide, sandy, and rimmed with bathers. In winter, only the most daring of big-wave riders challenge the largest rideable surf in the world. Waimea Bay is guarded by a Hawaiian temple on the Pupukea hillside.*

OPPOSITE: *Seemingly oblivious of stories of sugar's dismal outlook, the Waialua Mill grinds on. The mill and the company's acres of cane are the heart of the old plantation town, and its bread and butter.*

RIGHT: *Along Crozier Drive at Mokuleia, comfortable beachfront homes look out to the Pacific. The tiny community offers some unexpected activities. Here, polo players gather for a Sunday game, while gliders silently ride the thermals above Dillingham Field, Oahu's only soaring area.*

OPPOSITE: *Now cut off to wheel traffic by law and a huge landslide, rugged Kaena Point is a nature reserve. The western tip of Oahu, Kaena Point's finger of boulders and sand points northwest to distant Kauai.*

OPPOSITE: *An army of Hawaiian warriors once camped at Makaha preparing to invade the "separate kingdom" of Kauai. Today guests at the Sheraton Makaha Inn play the championship golf course in this dry Leeward valley.*

ABOVE: *Best known for its fishing, surfing,* luaus *and slack-key guitar music the community of Waianae on Oahu's Leeward coast staunchly retains its "local" lifestyle, although less than an hour's leisurely drive from Waikiki.*

RIGHT: *Climbing the southern slope of the Waianae range, Makakilo is a new bedroom community housing thousands of civilian and military commuters. Overlooking the Barbers Point Naval Air Station, Makakilo features brilliant sunsets.*

OPPOSITE: *Plantation life lives on at Waipahu town. The former one-crop town is a growing commercial and residential center overlooking Pearl Harbor.*

North of Wahiawa, between the Koolau and Waianae Mountains, are the U.S. Army's Schofield Barracks and the Wheeler Air Force Base.

Men of the battleship U.S.S. Arizona lie entombed beneath the white marble monument off Ford Island in Pearl Harbor marking the "Day of Infamy," December 7, 1941, that thrust the United States into World War II.

ABOVE: *Jets bearing the flags and logos of dozens of nations arrive and depart daily from Honolulu International Airport. The jet age gateway to the Hawaiian Islands receives up to five million visitors a year.*

OPPOSITE: *Early skippers rated Honolulu harbor the best in the Hawaiian Islands. From where a few grass shacks stood then, Honolulu has grown to become the mid-Pacific hub of government, finance and transportation.*

Restaurant Row and the Waterfront Towers are symbols of the new Honolulu. With a wide variety of international cuisines, Restaurant Row is a casual gathering place for city dwellers and visitors.

The upward flowing lines of the Hawaii State Capitol (center) suggest Hawaii's flowing waves and erupting volcanoes. In the foreground is painstakingly restored Iolani Palace, focus of the nineteenth-century Hawaiian monarchy.

OPPOSITE: *The National Memorial Cemetery of the Pacific in Punchbowl Crater honors more than 21,000 men and women who served in World Wars I and II, the Korean conflict and the Vietnam War. Dedicated in 1949, the cemetery's most visited grave is that of World War II combat-journalist Ernie Pyle.*

LEFT: *The green baseball diamond marks the University of Hawaii's Rainbow Stadium. More than 20,000 students attend classes on the 300-acre U.H. campus.*

ABOVE: *Rain showers drift down Manoa Valley from Manoa Falls to the University of Hawaii campus and out to sea at Waikiki. The upper valley receives up to 200 inches of rain in some years.*

OPPOSITE: *Serrated by time, wind and rain, the pinnacles of the Koolau Range provide a spectacular background to Honolulu and the windward side of Oahu. The Koolaus tend to block windward showers from leeward Honolulu and Waikiki.*

CHAPTER TWO

"Maui No Ka Oi," say long-time residents of the Valley Island. Newcomers agree. "Maui Is the Best."

The island's attractions range from the dry moonscape of Haleakala Crater to the rain forests of "heavenly" Hana on the southeast coast, and from staid Wailuku on the slopes of Puu Kukui to the "gold coast" resorts stretching from Napili to Makena.

Maui as we see it today was formed by the union of two of Hawaii's huge "shield" volcanoes. The older, Puu Kukui or West Maui Mountain, is the second wettest spot in the State with more than 400 inches a year. The mountains may once have reached 8,000 feet in height. Today, its eroded remnants constitute West Maui.

To the east lies the younger and taller Haleakala, "House of the Sun." Haleakala poured lava into the gap between the two volcanoes to form a single island, creating what is today probably the richest sugarcane land in the world.

On the isthmus are Maui's two principal commercial and administrative communities. Wailuku is the county seat. Kahului has the island's deep-water harbor, its airport, shopping malls, and a steadily expanding commercial/industrial complex.

The island's name originated in Polynesian mythology. Having pulled the island up from the sea bottom with his fish hook, the demigod Maui lassoed the sun as it raced past Haleakala and forced it to spend more time there so that his mother could dry her *kapa* (tapa cloth) properly.

PREVIOUS PAGES: *Misty rain clouds drift down the valleys of West Maui. These mountains are separate from those of East Maui, whose Haleakala rises to over 10,000 feet just above the clouds. Lava flows connected the two mountains.*

LEFT: *The sea cliffs of East Maui's Hana Coast were carved from Haleakala's lava by time, wind and waves, creating a series of tablelands laced with waterfalls cascading into the sea.*

Haleakala today offers an incredible vantage point for breathtaking views including spectacular sunrises and sunsets annually witnessed by thousands of visitors. The huge crater atop Haleakala is now a National Park. Its last eruption was in 1790.

Kipahulu valley stretches from the crater's eastern rim to the sea at the lovely Seven Pools. Not far from these natural swimming holes is the sleepy community of Hana, which can be reached by commuter plane or by the scenic, pot-holed and ever-twisting 50 mile Hana Highway from Kahului.

The small town lives up to its "Heavenly" nickname. Hana is an idyllic 15,000 acre cattle ranch, a luxury resort, and a community of closely knit families who enjoy a horse and buggy pace that other Hawaii residents envy.

On the lower slopes of Haleakala, above Kahului's broad sugar fields, are the cattle and truck farm communities of Maui. Cool Kula is famous for its flowers and sweet onions. Makawao, with weathered "Old West" wooden store fronts, annual rodeo and trendy restaurants, is a typical "up country" town.

The sunny leeward west coast of Maui is host to nearly two million visitors a year. Its heart, Lahaina, was once the capital of the Kingdom of Hawaii and the home of New England whalers and missionaries during the 1820s. Lahaina proper is mostly waterfront, four blocks deep and two miles long. Its streets today are lined with art galleries, restaurants and historic sites.

North and south of Lahaina, from Kaanapali and Napili to Wailea and Makena, resorts bloom on land covered just 30 years ago with sugarcane and thorny *kiawe* (mesquite) trees.

A plume of steam and the smell of crushed cane identify the Puunene Sugar Mill outside Kahului. As on other islands, sugar now ranks second to tourism in Maui's economy.

OPPOSITE: *Iao Valley Stream flows from Puu Kukui, the highest peak in West Maui, through Wailuku to the Pacific. Iao Valley Road follows the stream to a State park overshadowed by 2,250-foot Iao Needle, a volcanic pinnacle.*

ABOVE: *Staid Wailuku, the Maui county seat, rubs elbows with adjacent Kahului whose airport welcomes close to two million visitors a year. Once a missionary outpost, Wailuku today features historic buildings, parks and museums.*

ABOVE: *Quiet cane fields hide the historic past of Olowalu, between Wailuku and Lahaina, where in 1790 Hawaiians aboard a fleet of canoes massacred the crew of the American trading vessel* Eleanora.

OPPOSITE: *The tidy small-boat harbor at Lahaina reflects the days when whaling ships from New England wintered in the calm Lahaina Roads. Once the capital of the Hawaiian Kingdom, Lahaina today is a trendy art and visitor center.*

ABOVE: *Kaanapali resort was mostly covered with sugar cane in 1960. Carefully planned, Kaanapali is known for its fine hotels, championship golf courses, whaling museum, upscale shopping, and spectacular views of the nearby islands of Molokai and (opposite page) Lanai.*

Snug Kapalua befits its Hawaiian name, "arms embracing the sea." Once known as Fleming's Beach, Kapalua long has been a Maui favorite for picnics and swimming.

The Kahekili Highway circling West Maui grows rough and narrow near Kahakuloa Bay. Life in the isolated fishing and farming community moves at a slower pace than at towns down the road.

RIGHT: *A touring helicopter hovers at the base of Honokohau Falls near the northern tip of Maui. At Honokohau Bay the pavement ends and a rough dirt road continues to Wailuku.*

OPPOSITE: *Mount Eke with its unusual level summit, is the second highest peak in the West Maui Mountains. The unique swamp and bog at this isolated spot holds flora found nowhere else in the world.*

OPPOSITE: *Maui residents and thousands of visitors make pre-dawn pilgrimages up the switchbacks of Haleakala Crater Road to view incredible sunrises. Here, the Big Island is visible from the summit. Mountain bikers make the descent after arriving by bus.*

ABOVE: *The Kula district of Maui is famous for its sweet onions,* paniolos *(cowboys) and rural lifestyle. Commonly referred to as "Up Country," Kula spreads across the lower slopes of Haleakala above Wailuku and Kahului.*

OPPOSITE AND ABOVE:
Haleakala, "the house of the sun," is rich in Hawaiian legends. The moonscape scenery of the dormant volcanic crater seems to float over the island. During unusually chilly Hawaiian winters it can be snowcapped. Red Hill, 10,023 feet above sea level, is Maui's highest peak.

*Before windsurfing captured
the aquatic world's imagina-
tion and backing in the early
1980s, the old sugar-planta-
tion community of Paia (opposite) was known mainly for
having the last gas station on
the road to Hana. Today,
world windsurfing championships are often decided in
Hookipa's howling tradewinds
(above).*

The long, winding road to Hana (left) is renowned for its strenuous driving conditions and for the variety of its natural wonders like twin waterfalls (opposite), stands of giant bamboo, fern grottoes, and unpeopled valleys. Returning drivers often display souvenir tee-shirts that brag, "I Survived the Hana Highway."

73

ABOVE: *The Keanae Peninsula is a pocket of old Hawaii midway on the Hana Highway. Taro patches, a white church built in 1856, a Hawaiian community, and a pristine oceanfront location make Keanae one of the most scenic and historic stops on the long road.*

OPPOSITE: *"Heavenly Hana" includes Hana Bay, Kauiki Hill, the exclusive Hana Ranch Hotel, and the Hasegawa General Store. Hana is a slow-paced enclave of rural Maui life, rich in romantic beauty and peaceful isolation.*

OPPOSITE: *South of Hana, offshore from the village of Hokuula, sits tiny Alau island. A sailor's landmark, its wind and wave-eroded face epitomizes the geological history of Maui.*

ABOVE: *The fourth and fifth of the seven "sacred" pools of Kipahulu Valley south of Hana are just off the Hana Highway. Fed by the waterfalls streaming down the east slope of Haleakala, the pools offer a cool dip and a great view of the windward coast.*

RIGHT: *Kipahulu, Maui is a remote community at the end of the paved road past Hana and the seven "sacred" pools. The community is very sensitive about invasions of privacy by outsiders attempting to visit the remote gravesite of a famous American.*

OPPOSITE: *The isolated Manawainui valley, between Kipahulu and Kaupo, is normally dry. When the rain clouds of Hana reach the mountain peaks above the valley, this unique display will briefly appear.*

OPPOSITE: *Hikers today follow a path blazed by ancient Hawaiians through the Kaupo Gap, a massive slot in the rim of Haleakala Crater which allows foot passage from the Hana Coast to the central valley.*

ABOVE: *The walls of the Huialoha Church at windswept Kaupo are lava rock. The area bears the Hawaiian name Mokulau, "many islets," for the near-shore micro-archipelago of lava mounds there.*

ABOVE: *The long white sand beach at Makena was a popular destination for backpackers during the "hippy" 1970s. Despite the law, clothing wasn't always considered essential. Resort development now requires greater circumspection.*

OPPOSITE: *Boomerang-shape Molokini Islet is a short ride from Makena Beach. Charter boats daily bring scuba divers and snorkelers to explore Molokini's reefs and view Hawaiian marine life.*

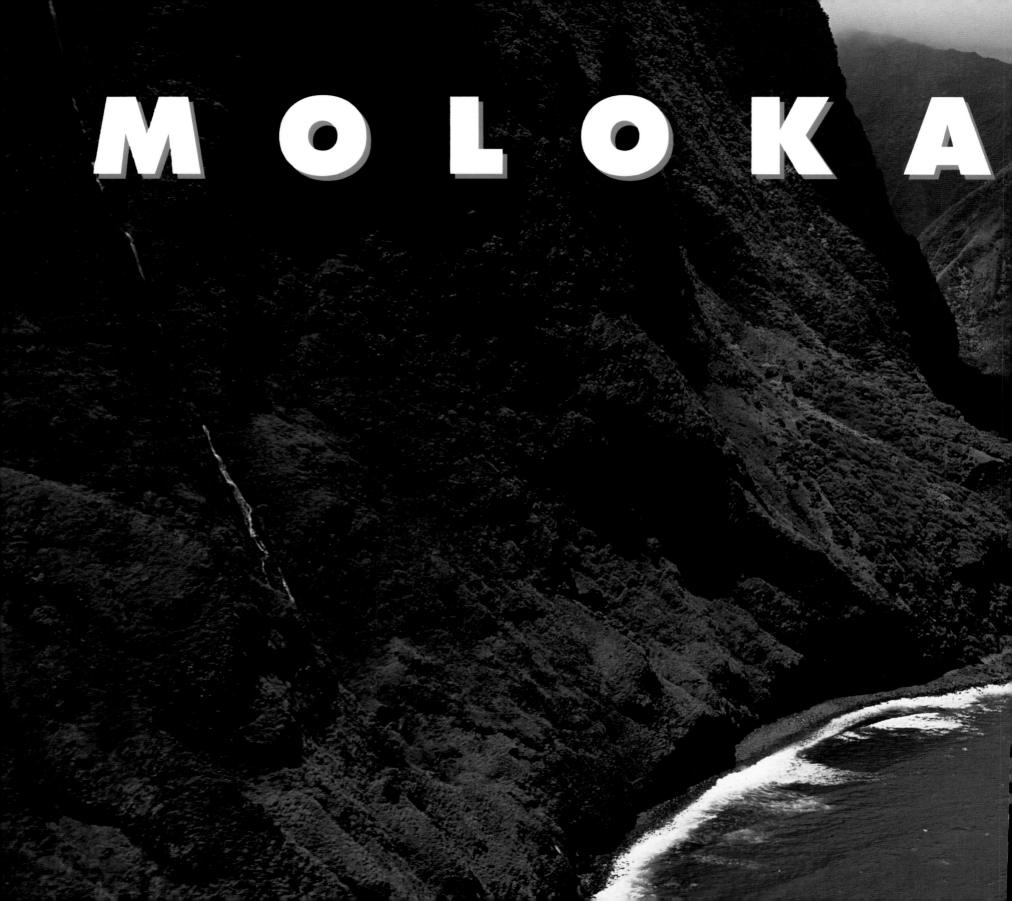

MOLOKA

I·LANAI

Slipper shape Molokai, 37 miles long and 10 wide, was the joint effort of three volcanoes. The infamous 25 mile wide Kaiwi or Molokai Channel separates it from Oahu, to which it ships beef, garden produce and highly prized watermelons.

A leisurely pace and warm aloha still characterize the "friendly island." Everything moves more slowly here. You get the feeling that every one of Molokai's 5,000 or so residents knows everyone else on the island.

Underlying this simplicity of life style is a rich and intriguing heritage. Archaeologists believe that isolated Halawa Valley on the northeast coast of Molokai was one of the earliest Polynesian settlements in Hawaii.

Westward along the precipitous coast from Halawa, in the shadow of mile-high Kamakou Mountain, are isolated Wailau and Pelekunu valleys, accessible only by sea or over a rugged, cliff-hugging trail. The coastline here includes the highest sea cliffs in the world. Although not as much visited as Kauai's famed Na Pali Coast, the north coast of Molokai is just as rich in Hawaiian legends and archaeological sites.

The cliffs end near Kalaupapa Peninsula where about 90 patients voluntarily remain at the nineteenth-century leper settlement made famous by the devoted work of Father Damien de Veuster.

Molokai's south shore has the remains of numerous pre-European fishponds, built as far back as the fifteenth century. The main street of sleepy Kaunakakai town at the island's center looks as if it had been carefully reconstructed as a movie setting.

PREVIOUS PAGES: *Although about half its length, the beauty of Molokai's little-explored north shore rivals that of Kauai's famed Na Pali Coast. Laced with cascades and waterfalls, Molokai's sea cliffs are the tallest in the world.*

LEFT: *Viewing the spectacular north coast cliffs of Molokai by helicopter is a one-of-a-kind experience. Unlike Kauai, Maui and the Big Island, Molokai has relatively few helicopters overhead.*

T he Largest Pineapple Plantation In the World" is the traditional description of 141 square mile Lanai. Soon the small, isolated island is likely to be better known for its luxury resorts.

Under a development plan introduced by Castle & Cooke, the owners of 98 percent of the island, new hotels are located at Manele Bay and on the plateau near Lanai's only airport, where commuter planes arrive from Honolulu, 65 miles away. New golf courses are in the works.

For a thousand years after the first Polynesians arrived in Hawaii, Lanai was uninhabited. Hawaiian legends say that ghosts and evil spirits roamed the island until the son of a Maui chief skillfully did away with them all. Only then did Hawaiians from Maui and Molokai settle here.

Lanai might have been the Salt Lake City of the Pacific if a Mormon settlement in the late 1800s had prospered. When it failed, the church moved its stake to Laie, at the northern tip of windward Oahu where the Mormon temple, Brigham Young University-Hawaii and the immensely popular Polynesian Cultural Center stand today.

In 1924 the face of Lanai changed with the planting of 15,000 acres of pineapple in the rich soil of the collapsed summit caldera of an extinct volcano. The island's only town, Lanai City, and a barge harbor were created at the same time. Lanai's pineapples go by barge daily to Honolulu. Many appear a few days later in California and East Coast supermarkets.

In the isolated valleys of North Molokai, Hawaiian families live much as their ancestors did. Supplies are brought in by small boats. Visitors are few.

ABOVE LEFT: *The pinnacles of Molokai's Pali Coast stand guard over secluded valleys. Kalaupapa Peninsula juts out in the distance.*

ABOVE RIGHT: *Siloama, Church of the Healing Spring, was built in 1871 for the lepers who literally had been abandoned at Kalawao, the original leper settlement on Molokai's north coast.*

OPPOSITE: *About 90 patients continue to reside at the leper settlement established in 1888 on Kalaupapa Peninsula, which is accessible today by commuter airplane, foot, or mule.*

UPPER RIGHT: *St. Philomena Catholic Church was completed in 1873. Here Father Damien de Veuster ministered to the lepers at Kalawao until he died of leprosy himself in 1884.*

LOWER RIGHT: *For Molokai's tiny population of 5,000 friends, Kaunakakai is "town." Most business and socializing is done along Ala Malama, the main street. Half-century-old wooden plantation buildings recall the days when pineapple was king.*

OPPOSITE: *Halawa valley is believed to have been the site of one of the first permanent Polynesian settlements some 1,500 years ago. A handful of farmers and fishermen now live where hundreds of Hawaiian dwellings once stood.*

OPPOSITE: *Formed by a single volcano, Lanai's highest point is 3,370-foot Lanaihale. About nine miles across the Lahaina Roads from Maui, once isolated Lanai is famous as the "pineapple island."*

ABOVE: *Luxury resort Koele Lodge, recently built by Rock Resorts, promises to change lifestyle on Lanai.*

ABOVE: *Prospects of plantation jobs in the "Pineapple Capital of the World" brought workers to Lanai from around the world in the 1920s. Harvesting these days is largely by summer-employed high-school students from the Western United States.*

OPPOSITE: *Lanai's tall Norfolk pines and cool upland climate traditionally have attracted hunters and anglers from Honolulu. Now a new luxury resort draws a different sort of visitor to the island.*

Hawaii's massive, diamond-shape "Big Island" is large enough to encompass all the other Hawaiian islands. Molten lava from Halemaumau's fiery pool in Kilauea Crater continues to spill into the sea, expanding the shoreline.

Geologically the youngest, the Big Island is the creation of five volcanoes. Two are especially impressive. Seasonally snow-capped 13,748-foot Mauna Kea, "the white mountain," towering over Hilo, would overshadow the Himalayas if measured from the ocean floor. Mauna Loa, the 13,680-foot "long mountain", is the most massive active volcano in the world.

From Kilauea at the heart of Hawaii Volcanoes National Park, visitors can hike over miles of marked trails, see an active lava flow, and spend the night at Volcano House, whose bath water is heated by the volcano.

Along the Big Island's leeward coast, a 60-mile stretch of luxury hotels attracts vacationers from around the globe with blue skies and ocean, world-class golf, and excellent deep-sea marlin fishing.

Situated on the oceanfront, Kailua-Kona is the heart of the Kona district. Missionaries from New England, the first to arrive in the islands, stepped ashore here in 1820 to be greeted by Hawaiian royalty. Hulihee Palace facing the small harbor recalls the days when the town was the administrative center of the Hawaiian Kingdom.

South of Kailua-Kona is Kealakekua Bay where Captain Cook died at the hands of the Hawaiians. An obelisk, erected by the British people, stands near the spot. The Kealakekua coral reefs offer some of the best

PREVIOUS PAGES: *Skiers on occasionally snow-capped Mauna Kea ride back to the top in four-wheel-drive vehicles. International teams of astronomers operate observatories on Mauna Kea's summit; the moisture-free atmosphere above 14,000 feet is excellent for the study of deep space.*

LEFT: *The ancient black sand beach at Kaimu in the Puna district has advanced inland a quarter mile in the past century. Now lava from Kilauea volcano creates new black sand beaches as it flows into the Pacific.*

POLOLU VALLEY
NORTH KOHALA
HAMAKUA COAST
WAIMEA
LAUPAHOEHOE
MAUNA LANI
WAIKOLOA
MAUNA KEA
HILO
KAILUA-KONA
MAUNA LOA
KEAUHOU
KILAUEA
KAIMU
KALAPANA

diving in Hawaii.

Ka Lai, or South Point, at the tip of the island is the southernmost point in the United States. Ka'u District has an unusual olivine green-sand beach at Punaluu. Ka'u also is a determined holdout against development. Life there goes on in the ways of old Hawaii.

Near the eastern tip of the Big Island, the village of Kalapana has been engulfed by Kilauea's lava in the longest running volcanic eruption in history. Lava oozing into the sea generates clouds of acrid steam.

"The Crescent City" of Hilo has the island's main airport and deep-water harbor. A lush and leisurely counterpoint to arid and hustling Kona, Hilo is a charming work-a-day town, the county seat and the Big Island's major population center.

Driving north of Hilo, motorists pass miles of Hamakua Coast sugar cane fields. As the industry wanes, the district seeks a future in diversified agriculture and small industries.

Just past sleepy Honokaa on the Hamakua Coast is awesome Waipio Valley. The steep road into the valley requires four wheel drive. The flat valley floor is a world of taro patches, lush vegetation and inky black ocean waves breaking over a black sand beach.

Inland and up from Honokaa is the *paniolo* (cowboy) town of Kamuela or Waimea. Nearly 3,000 feet above the coast and enjoying a climate akin to that of Northern California, Kamuela is a community of cattle ranchers and alternate lifestylers. Parker Ranch, where many of the cowboys work, is the largest privately owned cattle ranch in the nation.

North Kohala, at the northern tip of the Big Island, is emerald green. It is a world apart from the active volcanoes, dry forests and tourist enticements found elsewhere on the Big Island.

A bright rainbow colors the base of Akaka Falls north of Hilo. Rainbows frequently add splashes of color along the windward coast, especially early in the morning and late in the afternoon as water from inland rain forests cascades to the sea.

OPPOSITE: *Kilauea caldera's half-mile-wide Halemaumau crater fills with lava when Kilauea is active. Under its dark surface, lava reaches temperatures as high as 2,000 degrees Fahrenheit.*

ABOVE: *Pu'u O'o vent boils over from the heat of molten lava deep beneath Kilauea.*

Passengers aboard a helicopter watch red hot lava shoot straight up hundreds of feet above Puu O'o vent. This very active eruption draws thousands of people from around the world each year.

A circular hole bares the blazing heart of a lava tube. The tube carries molten lava farther down slope. As it pours into the ocean, the lava makes the Big Island bigger.

BEFORE: *This was the lush green coastline at the Puna community of Kalapana below the Kilauea volcano before the area was devastated by lava flows.*

AFTER: *May 1990—Kilauea lava spreads over Kalapana, destroying homes, businesses and local landmarks. The flow forced removal of the historic Painted Church, spared by a major 1977 flow.*

PREVIOUS PAGES: *Yachts anchor in Hilo Bay near Banyan Drive, the semicircular road around which Hilo's resort hotels are grouped. The Hamakua coast and Mauna Kea are a picturesque backdrop to Hilo.*

ABOVE: *Neat rows of homes line green and earth-red fields along the Hamakua coast north of Hilo.*

Quiet now, this aged mill once provided work for hundreds of Big Island sugar workers. Today macadamia nuts and other crops are gaining on sugar as major agricultural enterprises.

OPPOSITE: *Hamakua coast towns like Laupahoehoe remain much as they have been for generations. Named after the deep gulch in which it was built, the town is downstream from the rainy Laupahoehoe Forest Reserve.*

ABOVE: *Fed by rainfall on interior forests, Hamakua coast streams cascade through a series of pools and waterfalls to the sea.*

ABOVE: *Visible only from a boat or helicopter, towering cliffs and cascading waterfalls extend northward from the* taro *patches of Waipio to Pololu Valley in North Kohala.*

OPPOSITE: *Pololu Valley is partly filled with lava from an ancient eruption near Hawi in North Kohala. The valley marks the beginning of "civilization" along North Kohala's east side.*

Waimea, in the highlands of North Kohala, is often called Kamuela for Colonel Samuel ("Kamuela") Parker, early boss of the Parker Ranch. The town grew up around the headquarters of the enormous cattle ranch.

ABOVE: *Laurence Rockefeller built the luxurious Mauna Kea Beach Hotel in the late 1950s.*

OPPOSITE: *Restored natural fishponds line the lava-and-reef shelf fronting the Mauna Lani Resort. Its Francis Ii Brown golf course is among the most challenging in the world.*

OPPOSITE: *Swimming with dolphins and bathing in a series of turquoise beach-front pools are everyday doings at the new Hyatt Regency Waikoloa, one of the largest hotels in Hawaii.*

ABOVE: *The Royal Waikoloa is at Anaehoomalu beach, once favored by Hawaiian royalty. The Kings Trail, a footpath still visible along the leeward Big Island coast, runs through the property near ancient fishponds and petroglyph fields.*

On Keauhou Bay, south of Kailua-Kona, the Kona Surf Resort offers ocean and mountain views. It is surrounded by golf courses and tennis courts.

Stepping down to the sea at Oneo Bay just south of Kailua-Kona, the Kona Hilton's architecture reflects the slopes of Mauna Loa above the historic town.

KAUAI ◆

N I I H A U

Kauai is a 555-square-mile island whose shape is basically round. Residents and the more than one million visitors each year are largely confined to a coastal highway that stretches from Barking Sands on the dry west side to Ke'e Beach in lush Haena. Completing the circle between the two road ends is a foot path from Haena along the majestic Na Pali Coast as far as Kalalau valley. From that point to Barking Sands, access is only by boat.

From the dry plains of the west side, a great expanse of sugar cane blankets the island all the way to Anahola on the east. Near Kekaha, a second road winds upward along one rim of Waimea canyon to Kokee State Park and the fabulous Kalalau lookout. Lihue, the commercial center of Kauai, sits on a plateau above Nawiliwili harbor, which is the island's principal port. Kauai's main airport, largest shopping center and county seat are in Lihue.

On Kauai's south side, a world-class resort community has developed at Poipu. Past Lihue along the coastal highway, the rapidly growing communities of Wailua and Kapaa seem to be merging into one large resort town. Lush green Haena, Hanalei and Princeville at the northern end of the island have managed to maintain a rural atmosphere.

Kauai was called the "Separate Kingdom" because it was never conquered by Kamehameha the Great. The island became part of a unified Hawaiian Kingdom only through negotiations. The residents of Kauai still maintain a uniquely independent attitude.

PREVIOUS PAGES: *Waimea Canyon, the "Grand Canyon of the Pacific," slices through the hills above Barking Sands' long white beach on Kauai's west side.*

LEFT: *Passengers enjoy a superb view of the deep valleys and towering sea cliffs of Kauai's Na Pali Coast as their cruise ship circles Kauai.*

KILAUEA POINT

HAENA HANALEI MOLOAA BAY

NAPALI COAST

ANAHOLA

VALLEY OF THE LOST TRIBE

WAIALEALE

KAPAA

BARKING SANDS WAIMEA CANYON

WAILUA

LIHUE NAWILIWILI HARBOR

PUUWAI NIIHAU VILLAGE

WAIMEA LAWAI

HANAPEPE POIPU

It would have been easier for Captain Cook to visit Niihau in 1778 than for curious outsiders to do so today. The low, arid 73-square-mile "forbidden island" is *kapu* or off limits to everyone except its 300 or so native Hawaiian residents and guests of its owners, the Robinson family of Kauai.

Visible from Kauai's west side, and legally part of Kauai County, Niihau lies in the lee of Kauai's mountains which block the tradewind rain clouds that keep the Garden Island green.

Niihauans raise cattle and sheep, make charcoal from thorny *kiawe* trees, cultivate bees, and pick up tiny, colorful sea shells to string into Niihau shell leis, treasured by women of Hawaii and proudly worn at social functions.

In its isolation, Niihau retains a perhaps unmatched spirit of old Hawaii. Hawaiian remains the common language. An intact rural lifestyle is tied more closely to the nineteenth century than to the twenty-first.

Misty mountains behind the town help to make Hanalei Bay one of the most beautiful scenes in the Hawaiian Islands.

OPPOSITE: *Busy Nawiliwili harbor handles frequent cruise ships, inter-island barges, and Matson freighters. Facing Kalapaki Bay, the Westin Kauai at Kauai Lagoons Resort offers accommodation, shopping, and championship golf.*

ABOVE: *Set amid cane fields, Lihue is Kauai's county seat and commercial center. Over a million visitors arrive at Lihue Airport annually. The bulk of the island's freight comes through the port of Nawiliwili.*

ABOVE: *The Kauai Hilton and Beach Villas lies between Lihue Plantation cane fields and the Pacific. About midway between Lihue and the resorts at Wailua, the Kauai Hilton opened in the mid-1980s.*

OPPOSITE: *Kauai's* alii *(nobility) chose Wailua as their residence. Today, tour boats take visitors up the Wailua River to the Fern Grotto. Nearby is the venerable Coco Palms Resort.*

OPPOSITE: *The Wailua twin falls, north of Lihue, delight viewers who can drive to an overlook above the falls.*

ABOVE: *Nonou Mountain looks* makai *(seaward) toward the Sheraton Coconut Beach Hotel at Kapaa, the main community north of Lihue. The mountain is popularly known as the Sleeping Giant.*

A mostly Hawaiian community lives along the white sand beach at Anahola bay. A huge hole through the nearby Anahola mountains was the source of Hawaiian legends.

Quiet Moloaa Bay community still enjoys the serenity of old Kauai. Kuhio Highway passes papaya fields at Moloaa, but turns away from the coast where Moloaa's handful of residents live.

ABOVE: *For over 70 years, Kilauea Light guided ships past Kauai to and from the Orient. Today, Kilauea Point is a wildlife refuge, with the largest seabird colony in the main Hawaiian Islands.*

OPPOSITE: *The north coast of Kauai offers some of the most incredible scenery in all Hawaii. Known in old Hawaii as Halelea, "the house of pleasure," the coastline is a favorite of Hollywood film makers.*

OPPOSITE: *Waterfalls from Waialeale crater carry rain water from the wettest spot on earth to windward Kauai.*

ABOVE: *The homes and visitor accommodations at Princeville have panoramic views of ocean and mountains from a tableland 300 feet above the Pacific. The resort is outstanding for its 45 holes of championship golf.*

OPPOSITE: *The crescent bay at Hanalei is rich in scenery, surf spots and history. A rural Hawaiian lifestyle lives on here. Hanalei valley has the largest* taro *patches in Hawaii.*

ABOVE: *The blue water and coral reefs off Lumahai Beach, Wainiha Bay and Haena lead the eye to Mount Makana, which mature moviegoers recognize as Bali Hai in the 1950s musical,* "South Pacific."

FOLLOWING PAGES: *In summer, Kalalau beach is popular with backpackers and kayakers exploring the Na Pali coast. In winter, access to Kalalau beach and nearby Honopu valley is closed by huge waves.*

OPPOSITE: *Ocean mists shroud Kauai's Na Pali Coast accessible by helicopter or in inflatable boats when the surf is low, or on foot along the rugged Kalalau Trail.*

LEFT: *The fantasy setting of Honopu valley (foreground) and the Nualolo Aina hanging valley on the Na Pali coast fueled the fictitious 1920s "Legend of the Lost Tribe."*

OPPOSITE: *The beach dunes on Kauai's west side produce a distinctive "bark" when walked on. The sound gave its name to the beach, which runs from the sea cliffs at Polihale to Kekaha.*

ABOVE: *Red-dirt "cane-haul" roads in fields near Waimea form a petroglyphlike pattern when seen from the air.*

ABOVE: *Captain Cook's first Hawaii landing was at Waimea Bay, Kauai. The remains of a fort built for the Russians in the 1810s are across the Waimea River from a sleepy main street of shops and restaurants.*

OPPOSITE: *The multi-hue cliffs of mile-deep Waimea Canyon, the "Grand Canyon of the Pacific," provide an ever-changing pattern of colors in sun and shadow.*

OPPOSITE: *Olokele Mill, its fields, and the plantation homes of its workers stand together.*

ABOVE LEFT: *Kauai Electric Co., Port Allen and Hanapepe town form the commercial center of Kauai's west side.*

ABOVE RIGHT: *Visitors may tour the Allerton Estate and the National Tropical Botanical Gardens in lovely Lawai Valley. Rare tropical plants flourish here at the only tropical botanical gardens chartered by the U.S. Congress.*

ABOVE: *Where Hawaiian fishing villages once stood, Poipu Beach's sunny coves and beaches draw visitors to one of Kauai's major resort areas. Prince Kuhio, Hawaii's first Delegate to Congress, was born here.*

OPPOSITE: *A family* kuleana *(enclave) between Poipu and Nawiliwili, Kipukai is accessible only by a narrow road across the Hoary Head mountains.*

OPPOSITE: *Puuwai village is the population center of Niihau. Hawaiian is the main spoken language and entry is strictly limited.*

UPPER LEFT: *Tiny shells carefully picked along leeward beaches by the people of Niihau are strung into exquisite Niihau shell necklaces.*

LOWER LEFT: *The northern tip of Niihau is a long sand and lava point. Glass-ball fishing net floats, lost surfboards, rope and flotsam from ships and other islands are carried here by gusty trade winds and strong ocean currents.*

ABOUT THE PHOTOGRAPHY

This book is a result of my love of both photography and flying. I have been doing aerial photography in Hawaii for about 15 years and I still see something new every time that I go up. I will often tell my clients "What you really need on this job is an aerial shot." Even if maybe they don't. Sometimes it is hard to juggle my schedule, the pilot's schedule, and the weather to all come together at the same time. When it works, though, it is my favorite photography and just a lot of fun to do.

I did all the photos in this book from helicopters. The most important part of aerial photography is finding great pilots to work with. I had the help of many and want to thank: on Maui, Chuck Whiteman of AG Helicopters, Don Ballard of Hawaii Helicopters, Zac Baricuatro of Kenai Helicopters; on Kauai, Gardener Brown of Ohana Helicopters, Chuck di Piazza of Air Kauai, and pilots from Kenai Helicopters, South Sea Helicopters and Island Helicopters; on the island of Hawaii, William "Waili" Simon of Io Aviation, Kalani Ching of Kenai Air, David Okita of Volcano Helitours, and Jim Curtain of Kona Helicopters; on Oahu, Irwin Maltzman of Helicopters Hawaii, and Howard Esterbrook of Hawaii International Helicopters. I also especially want to thank H. D. "Woody" Wood & Robert Stanga of Makani Kai Helicopters for flying me in their Robinson 22 from the Napali coast of Kauai to the top of Haleakala, Maui and most places in between.

Of secondary importance is the equipment. Most of the photography was done with a Pentax 67 medium format camera. The lenses were 45mm, 55mm, 75mm, and 135mm.

Douglas Peebles

Photography by Douglas Peebles
Produced by Bennett Hymer
Written by Chris Cook
Editorial Assistance by
    Stuart Lillico

Art Direction and Design by
    Fred Bechlen and
    Leo Gonzalez
Design Assistants:
    Tamara Moan and
    Elaine Nakashima
Corporate Liaison: Galyn Wong

Typeset by Typehouse Hawaii
Headlines: Futura Extra Black
Text: Baskerville Roman
Captions: Baskerville Italic

Printed and Bound in Hong Kong
    by Everbest Printing Co., Ltd.